# Night Physics

# NIGHT Physics

## M. Travis Lane

BRICK BOOKS

CANADIAN CATALOGUING IN PUBLICATION DATA

Lane, M. Travis (Millicent Travis), 1934-
  Night physics

Poems.
ISBN 0-919626-70-X

I. Title.

PS8573.A55N5  1994    C811'.54    C94-930387-9
PR9199.3.L35N5  1994

The support of the Canada Council and the Ontario Arts Council is gratefully acknowledged. The support of the Government of Ontario through the Ministry of Culture, Tourism and Recreation is also gratefully acknowledged.

Some of these poems have previously appeared in: *The Antigonish Review, The Canadian Forum, The Cormorant, The Dalhousie Review, Existere, The Moosehead Anthology, Northward Journal, The Southern Review.*

Cover art is after a woodcut by Brigid Grant.

Typeset in Trump Mediaeval, printed and bound by The Porcupine's Quill. The stock is acid-free Zephyr Antique laid.

Brick Books
Box 38, Station B
London, Ontario
N6A 4V3

# Contents

I   Fall-Winter 1990-1991 9

II  Half Past 19
Here: 20
Homage to First Principle 21
'Beginning the World' 23
The Stars Perspire 25
Pottage 26
The Deputy 27
Having Traveled to the Moon ... 28
I Am the Cross of Mirrors 29
Night Physics 30
Husks 31
The Thing Outside 32
Eyefall 33
The Bell 34
Rainbow for Netty Myer 35
My Line Has No Hook 36

III  Anachronistic Gnat Music 39

IV  'Come Up and Be Dead!' 57
Everything's Just Fine 58
Music for a While 60
Just Like That 61
Triptych/Tock 62
Bog Song 65
Ugetsu 66
'Woman with Child' 67
AFrom the Wings 68
About the Size of It 69
Postcard from Yellowstone 70
Too Close for Comfort to the Text 71
'Woman with Green Umbrella' by Van Gogh 72
O 73
Katy's Cove 74
There Are Real Ants in the Metro 76
Consider Briefly 77
Seven Classical Chinese Pictures 78

*to the Voice of Women for Peace, Fredericton branch*

I

## Fall-Winter 1990-1991

1  On the newly dug tulip bed
the cemetery kitten rolls, its paws
powdered with soil. Its collar says
'I am cared for.' Just beyond
the bulb plot is the monument
for soldiers killed in action –
rubble, beneath a scrabble of vines,
replaced now by a single stone, smooth,
shiny, and grey as a credit card.

Some of them never fired their guns.
How do we know where the devil is?
For all I know, shinned up that shabby fir tree,
grey tail jerking against its bark,
greedy, noisy, half-blind with age.

This constant talk of war seems like
the tinfoil pennants a garage
sets out for new sales (secondhand):
'Come die for your country somewhere else!'
all rustle and glitter. Not in
this tidy garden where the graves
are calm as a motel carpet when the guest's
checked out, the bed made up.

Think of the mosses on these stones,
how long they took. That ivy, no short work
breaking those boulders.
War kills the future sooner than the past,
but time takes time.
We could well wait the devil out.
Why push?

2 Dry winter. The brown, pale field
  incised by paw and hoof some months ago
  reads like an outdated schedule
  of long-ago departures. At its crest
  a thin pine flares its eagle-wing
  green head-dress like a warrior's.
  At its foot, the felled kin lie,
  corded and tallied.

  So still, so motionless it seems
  as if the ice-clay earth won't turn,
  or the long shadows lengthen their pale thatch.
  And yet the east, without a cloud,
  has darkened as I watch. Small things
  may find a respite in the dusk, and I,
  perhaps. Is all this barren beauty
  half a lie? The shaggy marsh
  with its dismantling ice-panes, nests
  of twigs and rotting logs
  beyond that empty crescent where the sky
  and this grey highway make a bond,
  still marks a passage, not a past.
  This bare field is no desert.

  And yet the plow may be retoothed,
  the pennants felled, and dragons sown,
  tilled, sown again, a harvest
  of new death.

3 What will console us now?
Not those teen-talking men
who eyeball, instead of looking. Who see death, send
others off to die. Not those machines
that can't see people on the ground,
nor soldiers, honest, ignorant.
Evil does evil in return.

What time and commerce could achieve,
relieving the yearnings of the poor
for tyrants to make hatreds into strength,
we will not know.
Even the devil has somewhat on his side.
We can't see straight if we don't blink,
pause, wonder, even hesitate.
Nothing is all that simple.
Nothing is all that straight.

4 A radar-crested yellow bird hunts me.
I hide in a glass forest
crackling with static, electric hail.
I am lost in a white-out desert – dunes,
wind-pits, water-holes
where the blue flicker of a breath
could catch a bird eye –
                                    let me sink
into the sand like a beetle, hooded,
heat-goggled, antennae drawn
back, floundering –
                              the smoke
drifts toward me, ancient, potent,
whining.
Let me hide under a mullein leaf –
                    off camera.




5 Young dogs romping in the snow
with dolphin leap, sky-wag, tar-yellow eyes
clear with the noon of innocence,
naive and handsome –

How they run and run and whirl about!

And we will find
tomorrow, if they're not leashed in,
among our small plantation of young spruce,
the gashed ribs of a pregnant doe, and she

also leaped lovely, as innocent, naive.

6   A tear drop hangs from the beak of a bird.
    It is never enough.
    What is a true religion! God
    desires no deaths!

    God's blessing would turn our hands to grass,
    but this black rain
    will rot us where we plant
    without God's blessing, patience, our rock breasts.



7   Fluish and sick with listening to the news
    I feel as if I were about
    to float away and be nowhere.

    But you, pert corporal Patsy on the screen,
    have done just that.

    I can not grab you and pull you out –
    and you have turned into a photograph,
    framed, on a table by the couch
    where the afghan is still spread
    to keep your old dog's hair off the rubbed plush.

    Your sunflower smile will dazzle me years,
    years after the life you did not have
    has grown grey in your mother's scrapbooks.

    Where had you volunteered to go?
    It was 'only a job' you said. Honey.
    You weren't 'only' to us.

8  When you walked up that stair I lost your sight.
Your back was erased when they latched the door.
What should I whisper to myself
from your cold bedside?

I can't believe what you believed, or had to.
You are coin they notch in a meter, so much time,
that gone, they spend
somebody else.

I have lost your eyes, your nervousness
in company, your jokes,
the red mud on your socks.

Someone was drowning; they threw you in
weighted with cannon round your neck.

A game of cards.
They were gambling.


9  The street is still light, and the windows gleam
yellow against the snow-blued sky.
Home-time. The offices will close, the street lights shine out
    stronger, while, indoors,
hearing my old dog murmur in her sleep
as if she were afield and young,
hearing the leaf-fall footsteps of the squirrels,
I could be so content –

as if this weather floated without wind
along a darkening river.

                    But
below the satin polish of the keel
the kelp heads of drowned soldiers bob.
The distant shore
seems lined with haggard refugees whose cold
untented hands
could pierce my comfort like ice spears, but
they *are* far –
                    This boat
moves on its errands, passive as a dream
within a dream, as if they were not real,
those maimed and whispering orphans,
those beacon-traced fire-arches over their plains.

Does evil need this evil?
Life after life folds over like the leaves
of an unending story in a book
that no one reads but wind which tears
and tatters every page.

    The street is still light, though darker, and the bus
    has dropped its last two passengers. Across the way
    the college chapel's cross has caught
    the first faint dustings of fresh snow.
    We can't undo what has been done. What now?
    The 'other way,' ignored, untried, invisible,
    still waits.

## Half Past

This is the place where the map gives out,
worn in its folds, as it long has been.

Your label's thin (mother/daughter/
sister/wife) and everywhere
an equal sky
fills the unstable woods.

Your shadow lags
as if you could step out of it.
What's left? The work
you thought your best, like a blazed stump
in a logged pasture, can not call
your footsteps to it.

Half past midlife you find yourself
in a rough barren where no trees
or brambles block your way.
There is no path. Whichever way
you turn will be toward darkness.

Choose. The plot
of your unworded story is your own.
Or have the path
and you run out together,
overgrown, emplaced?

Will the horizon part, or a long stair
come down from those clouds, mountainous,
that pass and pass and never speak?

Write everything. These minutes are your own.
Business-arising has been paid
to each according to her need
(and you need nothing).

No map, no compass, and no plan.
There is, still, light.

**Here:**


A deep, white granite portico:
its pillars are pale grey
like cedar trunks, or like
Greek columns in the sea, immersed
in a soft mist that comes
in like a curtain, aqueous,
from the green, moss-barked citrus trees
in their stone urns. The afternoon
coils from the slatted benches as if it
had dozed among the scented leaves
til the slight shuffling of the wind
had wakened it. The mist
encloses the deep valley
which contains
the orchards, the white portico,
its antique columns, graven stones;
and this porch
holds all of this together in
two minutes of your breathing.
You may rest here, while you read here.
Sit down and have some coffee.
I'll be back.

**Homage to First Principle**
– Taoist wall paintings at the Royal Ontario Museum

The stillness of the upper night
where all things move

by their progression distanced from
our human greed and fury
is the gods

as we can yet imagine them:
star charts, mathematic sentences,
blue mandalas of the way
whose inward state the eye
sees only as a compass out of time

in time.

And yet it moves

as this dull marble terra moves
upon which our commotion: dust,
the glittering mica of the sea,
half tears, half dung,
seems a perverse refusal to take form.

A petty chaos,
yet our will
strives ever toward their majesty,
which in its other world, our own,
is blinded by eternal light:
indifferent, undiffering,
heads whorled with human attributes,

Lord of the Northern Dipper,
Jade Emperor, the
compassionate First Principle
that we suppose.

Against the eggshell of our cave
   the frescoes form:
          head-dress, tiara,
  silken robes – reds, greens, blue-greys –

Its walls grow holy with our art, our
   homage
         to First Principle.

## 'Beginning the World'

First burial: my doll. The second
this grey blanket shrouding sight.
Between them runs the jolting coach
where God, the eccentric gentleman,
hurls the uneatables away.
The fog turns brick, 'particular.'
There are no explanations. God
imposes his summer face on all.

Nameless my father, unnameable
my mother, winter's daughter I:
old woman of the dirty sky.
In the unthawing garden of my birth
I buried my only, truest friend
who, with her cloth heart, loved me most.
She will not rise up.
I have wept too long.

The locked doors rattle against the flowers
of this shut bower; the velvet grey
forget-me-nots like mouse-paws and the pale
wallpaper ferns like broom-straws, white
crumpled roses like handkerchiefs
or children's hands, grubby at railings.
The key slips, clinking on its wards.
Against the keyhole, their dear demands.

The sun turns its scarlet finger on the blinds
and slides away to its cranny,
guardian uncomfortable, east rising,
westering despair.
Orphans like cracker crumbs cling to his vest,
or like unfledged, weak sparrows chirp for bread.
They can't fly out. My keys
shut up the housekeeping.

God scowls in his pink scowling place
like a disappointed baby.
When the locked door opens, the letters melt,
and the seal of the box is broken,
judgement be given – hope,
youth, folly, and old age
escape, will be eaten up –
and constant fog.

This fever veils my midnight. All the time
I practiced in the mirror the doll stare,
beloved, unjudging, listening –
my rose complexion is cast away,
wracked up. The growing darknesses
break up the confines of my face.
I am a paper flower, a glass case,
stone casket, sentence long deferred.

My mother, ice throne melting, breaks.
I was born dead, but in this birth
begin again another world
with my drowned lover.
Like waters covering the fields
which move outside my history
I sink beyond all sentences
and slip, through locks, to sea.

## The Stars Perspire

The stars perspire,
go in and out of living like small bugs.

An absence like a stone door
stands between.

You put your hand up to it, and it drains
your body heat.

> Eat it like snow.
> You will die of it.

Against this wilderness, this plain
forgetfulness, a bird

from the dim rafters of its tree
poses its miniature machine,

> its sweat,
> its tiny voice.

**Pottage**
– for Willi Paynter, 3 weeks

It's real. You can warm your hands on it.
Smell it, it's good: a dish of plums
or the sea in its roof-tiles sparkling
or swan in a cold mirror full embraced,
or you,
round-eyed, and staring at a world
not yet deciphered,
new –

your hands like the leaves of a violet –

    In the monkey house the lemurs stared
    (I could not entertain them long.)
    Poor heroes, tiny in their myths –
    like the oriole
    who wakes me before dawn to say
    'It's me, me, mine!'

    The 'other' world
    bobs like a sea beast under waves;
    it may be there.
    It's this world, warm,
    delectable,
    this one
    I want.

At your mother's face
you lick your lips.

**The Deputy**
– for E.W.T.


You are always on everyone's side,
like God. Too moderate. It makes me cross,
sometimes. But now,
remembering how you used to feed
the crippled, one-eyed gator
with dog biscuits – you'd stand
above him on the bridge
and throw food down toward his good eye,
with the clustering fish on his other side
popping the water for the crumbs,
and the little boys
at the landing with their crablines
who poach bass
from the pond, late evenings, when
all that the dog can do is bark –
they think you don't know that they do –
I wish your moderation
for us all.


You put out trash for the raccoons
and pull the dog from battles by his leg.
You watch cardinals and nonpareils
with the cat and listen for
spring peepers, mark
the first gold jasmine in the pines.
Nothing surprises – the magazines
with violent opinions, friends,
the strange ways of relations.
And today
you count the ducks out on the marsh.
One's missing,
not the one with the broken wing,
but another.
    Someone
keeps track of things.


How could God count His sparrows
without you?

**Having Traveled to the Moon**
**Through the Wise Distillation of Dew**

The clarity of those two men of de Bergerac's,
transported to the moon, who speak
as you and I might, prisoned in a glass,
two moon beams:

All those stupid eyes
trained on us, dazzling peerers, who can't see,
learn what we do not say, perceive
what we are not,
and we

being within the privacy
of lucid thought
consort, a marriage of pure mind, a dignity
beyond the costume fur, flesh, fin,
they see of us.

We breed
ethereal distillations like the ones
which brought us here,
like dew
which, rising into clouds, grows thinner,
higher, lighter,
as we do.
We shall turn into light,
in time.
As did
de Bergerac.

Was it his light we loved him for,
or his shade-casting prominence?
Perhaps his loony creatures were correct:
outsides are all that matters.
Would the nose
be nothing if not heavenward its breath,
as on these windy winter days,
casts its white plume, grotesque?

## I Am the Cross of Mirrors

I stand between two mirrors; they reflect
each other.

Their lights cross, close.
A door
they are to inner light
the outer fire.

The door
of mirror into mirror is ajar,
not open, never fully so –
the lights would kill me,
trembling in their cross.

A child's hand holds them open.

I stand between two mirrors; they reflect
each other.

A swallow flies from the sundial, leaves
a shadow; lighting, leaves
a leafless shade. It is all light,
in the swallow's eye.

The mirrors shatter daybreak.
Darkness flies
into the sun which is its nest, which is
all mirrors crossing in one place. I burn.

I am the cross of mirrors, door to light –
not open, but a small child's hand
keeps it ajar.

Jar, light, a waterglass of flame –
I burn. The swallow sings.
I am the cross of mirrors,
door to light.

## Night Physics

The curves of the ticking sky-hole
that pull together the plumbed abyss –
or the concentrate
in a hurt eye –

astound the night's astronomers.

Great sizzling fires move motionless,
soundlessly swimming
even –

as dark hides darkness –
or as light

hides light –

## Husks

The wet seed freezes in the tin
that dangles from the clothesline for the birds.
The pond is agate. The red haws
of the rugosa spice the air. A squirrel,
three-legged and Ethiopian-eyed, wags their spiked wands.
The street lights fur the garbage bins
(emptied last night). His scraping paws
turn over the tatters of the lawn
for some forgotten miracle –
shards, shards . . .

Upon such husks support a mind
that feels the night come on like snow
hiding the marks and tracings of the past,
all maps of wrong maze turnings, dangerous trails,
all turnings towards amnesia, towards
the cosy cavern, trap
of what we do not know
and sleep in, knowing time dispels
the need of what we can not find:
words, words.

## The Thing Outside

A desperate unhappiness lies hereabouts;
like a house pet wants in, wants out, or
courses the back streets, but
nothing diverts its focus long –
neither the moon
whose laden finger stripes the house
nor the attention of a friend
drowning nearby, but swimming hard.

I close my doors.
Its voice comes in the window,
short of breath,
catching its words as if they hurt.
I leave a bit of chopped food on the step.
Almost enough. It grabs and runs.
It's crouching under the bushes there.
It would overwhelm me like a sea
in which I do not choose to swim.
Like Noah on his splinter, I'm afloat.
Like Noah's wife
I tip my glass.
                'Cheers!' I say
to the dark outside. And the darkness
whispers back.

**Eyefall**

A large window looking out into the valley
with the leaves all falling

they fall
and the wind runs down the hills
and the long, low valley

this box is not this window
these four walls

but the shut doors of eyefall
where I walk

I have no shadow, make no noise
leaves, bending at my footstep, rise again

> '*My dearest dear, I am not here,*
> *but only in your heart.*'

## The Bell
– for H.M.L.

The children in the timbered tower
swung from the bell rack; their voices belled
the cross beams where the great voice hung,
fell, and was silent.

Below the tower
the village blossomed in the mist,
pale, early buds. The yellow moss
gilded the sagging, raftered church
whose heavy clock
echoed across the valley the long strokes
the children rang above it in the tower.

The bell rack made a crucifix
above the cramped, black oubliette.
Wild flowers hung
along the dripping window sills,
draining the rock for their livelihood.

You also bloomed at the tower's rim,
pale as the orchards cloudy in the fields,
and made a silent music in the stones.

And that was years, was years ago.
The bell of Caesar's tower has no tongue.
All history is dead, stone dumb.
Life, only,
is.

**Rainbow for Netty Myer**


Of the photograph you sent me once:
a hiker in shadows, and something in her hands –
a book, a pail of water, solitude –
I remember mostly shadows and the snow
whose rainbow crystals marked the road
across a white field: silence shared
with wilderness, a listening.

Here the rain
that drummed the river meadows has gone on,
and there's a double rainbow. Double-ringed
the coarse, logged fields, and the glacier stones.
Ducks, swallows, midges: afternoon
repeating a promise.

Silence is gold at the rainbow's end.
You can carry it:
all that a poem can never say:
*your life, your life.*

**My Line Has No Hook**


My line has no hook.
You must swim up to it with your bare hand.
Let it curl like a vine around your thumb.

I, too, am naked.

III

**Anachronistic Gnat Music**


The Conventions: Three Kings (Them): Groucho
Chico
Harpo
Prince (Him): Pierrot, Peter Pan
Princess (Her): Pierrette, Wendy
Poet (Us): Papageno
Muse (It): Pegasus
Dog (Dog): Sirius


*Prelude*

The theatre in darkness.
Stars
slowly: Venus, Mars, Aldebaran –

the Milky Way
mists over the proscenium.
The staging drifts a little on that flow.

The constellations we pick out are blurred,
uncertain, fabulous –
until the moon,
as local as a street lamp,
blots them out.


*I : i  Analectic Nook Music*

A forest made of paper, or
a raft set up with potted trees, or
Huck's log home (cut lumber on a current). We're
bewildered: night, woods, Heraclitean flux.

The moon's shrunk to a spotlight, and the faint
arch of the stars returns, at intervals,
as if clouds sometimes intervene.

Untethered on the wobbly stage,
a packhorse. Seated, the Poet with his corn-
cob flute, and, standing, the Prince
(Tom Sawyer acting him) and dog
(a border collie) and,
spread out by the prompter's box,
the Book.

The spotlight crowns the Prince. (The Prince,
perhaps, has chosen to be crowned.)

*Prince:* 'Poet, awake!
    From the bathetic forests of your mind
    you must invent my glory, my
    solution to the voicelessness of sky.
    I am God's germ!'

*Poet:* 'You're who?'

*Prince:* 'I'm your construction. I'm your words,
    your definitions, your imprints,
    your homoname.'

*Poet:* 'A kind of walking thesaurus –
    a monster who begins
    before I write and keeps on
    when I drop the pen.'

*Prince:* 'Before hand and behind hand, I'm
    eternal. Poetry's not passing time
    but keeping it.
    Derry da or derry down. Tick tock.'

Flute music. The horse (inflated sheet, four sneakers,
a dubious stability) bobs at the Poet's shoulder as he plays.
The dog perks up. The music moves the raft.

The spotlight turns like an airport's beam
and, searching the backdrop, fastens on
a tiny light –
        *zooms in:*

match flame –
a chicken coop on fire –
a city through a telescope –
a comet's eye
whose tail, peacocked with irises
sweeps suburbs, an imperial robe which
flaring toward the orchestra, surrounds us, fades,
invisible –
    and leaves the stage, mid-city,
neoned midnight. Newsprint leaves,
torn posters, poles instead of trees. A hotel,
engulfing, like a giant's mouth,
swallows the stage.

We are
mid-lobby. Trees in pots again. Chairs, tables.
At the back
three men are playing euchre. (Curls,
moustaches, long pale overcoats.)
The dog lifts a leg,
then settles by the prompter's box and stares,
a shepherd's eye on the Milky Way.

### I : ii  Agon Clinic Nut Music

The Poet deflates the horse, collapses it,
and folds it into a parcel.

*Poet:* 'Shall I book us rooms? Page someone?'

*Prince:* 'The night's still young. The game's afoot.
  Et cetera, et cetera.
  When the music falters I must quote.
  What a penpal you are! Out of ink?'

*Poet:* 'The system is a little down.'

*Prince:* 'Well, rev it up.' (He kicks the horse.)
   'A poet ought to be inspired.
   Here is a forest of images' (he waves his hand)
   'among which real ideas move.
   Those men, perhaps, you've stationed at the back?'

*Poet:* 'The realm of the subconscious. The three kings:
   Balthazar, Kaspar, Melchior,
   if you'll take their word.
   Or Peachum, Lockit, Filch.
   The wisemen with their starry gaze,
   they'll lead you on.
   I'd rather eat.'

*Prince:* 'How plebian.'

*Poet:* 'I can't write on an empty stomach.'

*Prince:* 'You need a firmer muscle tone.'

*Poet:* 'I mean I'm ventriloquial.
   Look, go away. Go bother them.
   Go ask them to set you up somehow.
   They know all motives, basic plots.'

*Prince* (miffed, but willing to act on the suggestion):
   'Gentlemen, a word with you.
   Can you assist
   me and my servant, this belly-brain?'

The three kings rise in unison: 'Good evening.'

*Groucho:* 'What do you want?'

*Prince:* 'Meaning. Heroic action. Fame!'

*Poet:* 'A nominative case. I,
   a common denominator, can only verbalize –
   hotels instead of palaces
   and knaves instead of kings!'

*Prince:* 'Be serious!'

(The dog pricks its ears, as if its name were called,
but, perceiving its error, returns to astronometry.)

*Poet:* 'He wants a linear narrative.
　　　From here to there,
　　　wherever here or there may be.'


## *I : iii  Aching Back Knot Music*

*Groucho:* 'Do you feel lost? No star to guide?
　　　Each crevice of the night sky burns
　　　with messengers and charlatans.
　　　You make the figures that you see, and I,
　　　sky-pilot, shall instruct
　　　you, Prince, invented Hero, and ignore
　　　you, Papageno, who invents
　　　as I, one day, invented you.'

*Chico:*　I'm the Doctor. Anything
　　　you want I fix. My sonic tool,
　　　my bag of Ariadne's string,
　　　my candy for the natives' (he displays
　　　them) – 'This guy's my pal, the Harlequin,
　　　who, only speaking music, can not lie.
　　　We're at your service. Trust
　　　me. Trust the Captain. We're the crew.
　　　We sell insurance also. All you do –
　　　is ask.'

*Harpo:* (*Lamb-eyed, a glutton for gold girls,
　　　a Joseph's coat, a tartan of significance, I have
　　　no words, I am pure music. Call me Light
　　　and I will leave you lighter . . .*)

*Groucho:* 'I'm the Captain. He's the Doc.
The mute's my bagman, courier.
I make your luck. Doc fixes if he can.
And in the emptied box, your life,
music is left, your light motif,
til it runs out . . .'

*Poet:* 'Ping, Pang, and Pong.'

*Prince:* 'Stop calling names.'

*Groucho:* 'Power, glamour, victory
against the mediocrity
of cowardice or poverty!
Fist at the ready, you'll control
all that might oppress your soul!'

*Chico:* 'Money, money, money
casts a spell.
Money, money, money
makes you well!'

He tosses sequins, like flaked lights
or bees in swarm, small flecks of fire.
The Harlequin's bag trousers swell
and suck them in.

*Groucho:* 'Let me show you our maps.'

*Chico:* 'Prospectuses.'

Harpo flashes open his overcoat, showing a postcard
pinned inside.

*Groucho:* 'Your mission won't be easy. Night
will fill your mind with fears and doubt.
Wild birds will utter nonsense in the trees
and north seem false to magnet.
Be deaf to idle chatterers. Be cunning,
steadfast, silent as a stone!'

*Poet:* 'Silence is not my discipline.
You shut my mouth,
my belly grumbles just as loud.'


*Prince:* 'Ssshhh.' (Scowls at the poet, takes the maps, eyes
briefly the closed overcoat, then, head erect
and noble, exits off.)

*Poet:* 'Go, go, my prince, my literature,
my fib. You have the noble mind of art
and will not think of bed when glory lurks
like a lamed panther, fabulous
and probably extinct, except
for prints I sometimes think I see –
a smell of death – But heroes can not die.
They fade away!'


## II : i  Erl König Echt Music

A city park. A little pond in the distance
which reflects the moon. Stage front:
a small gazebo needing paint.
The Princess, who will not
be rescued by the hero but,
chatting with the handyman
has made herself handy and escaped
from what Pandora's box the plot
invented for her. Possibly
the Poet, tired of the Prince,
skipped half a chapter, let her out
upon her own recognizance.

They are picnicking by candlelight.
(The dog's not moved; its nose is on its paws.)

*Princess:* 'I was born maimed in dreamtime, and my hands
   undo the things they fabricate.
   I pick up his messes and I mend
   his socks, his shirts, his alibis.
   My part is badly written. No grand deeds –
   just patience and endurance. What a bore!
   Besides, you make me double-faced: Odette/Odile,
   or Columbine who's also aquilegia, an eagle-dove,
   hag-maiden, Wendy who enslaves, whose mothering
   means growing up, a death.

   'Yet you're the only friend I have. You sympathize.
   Sit by me on the blanket. Sing of love,
   of home, of happy days.
   The Prince has his get-rich schemes.
   He won't talk to me. You, ignorant, loutish,
   cheer me up. Explain the plot.
   I like your explanations, though
   I can't say I accept them.'

*Poet:* 'Yours is a better part than his.
   He sounds like such an idiot.
   Yet you are each the other's half.
   (Things only come in twos or threes
   in stories.) You both are me.
   Except I'm only half myself.
   My better half, the shadow of my mind,
   slips behind me when I turn to look at it
   as if my look would hurt it, or as if
   I had no shadow, am no thing.

   'The Prince is me as hero: you
   me as the heroine. You've more of me,
   being house-bound, except you are
   too fine, too pure, too papery.
   The egg that held you had no yolk.'

*Princess:* 'A piece of you, the other side of him?
　　A sort of royal turtle dove, a hen
　　to his sun-daring rooster, like a shade
　　defined by light, no thing
　　but contrast, opposite, Yang's Yin?
　　What tosh!
　　A princess has a grandeur of her own.
　　Valour, adventure, suffering!
　　I force him to find truth where truth is hid,
　　and somewhat doubt he'll find it, though I hint.'

She opens the picnic hamper and dumps in
the emptied thermos, paper plates; takes out
three gussied boxes, 'He must choose.'

*Poet:* 'Not yet. The kings control him. We
　　are backdrop for his theatre, and you must grow
　　from chrysalis to Luna til it is
　　your beacon lights him through the woods,
　　the flames, the battles, later on.
　　I can not think you further. You must go.'

She rises, snuffs the candles, and goes off.

*Poet:* 'Lead's the right choice. For silence is
　　golden and speech silver. Lead
　　is death. Mortality means life,
　　which means a choice.
　　He chooses her.
　　A poet chooses to be frog.
　　A kiss would make me nothing but myself.'

## II : ii  Epic Clammy Newt Music

Alone in the gazebo in the dark,
the Poet looks cold. The stars are bright
and something like a lantern in a tree,
or a white balloon some child has lost,
is all we have to see by. Mist,
soft as cygnet feathers, creeps
like frosted breath across the stage.
Crepuscular music might be guessed.
The Poet fetches out his flute.
Slowly, the horse inflates itself.

### The Song of the Imitation Horse
### in Its Flat-Footed Pasture

*Pegasus:* 'Believe me, for the moment.
   My four feet
   are not in their construction hoofed
   as I pretend them, and my back
   wobbles beneath no burden but
   the sheeting on it. I support
   the plot. You have no other plot
   than this: the good's besieged,
   the bad ones seem to win,
   the kind horse helps.

   'I am that thing
   in nature you make use of,
   in your kin
   you take for granted. I am what
   depends on a construction in your mind,
   a beast and a collusion in the flesh,
   two-fleshed – a beast with one back
   which is sheet
   and more heads than are thinking.

   'Wings are mine,
   your Pegasus.
   I fly no higher than you do.'

## II : iii  Minor Kleenex Sniff Music

Same set. A night bird's cry, leaves rustling.
The dog, asleep, is a dark shadow only.
The horse is folded up again.
The poet blows his flute, but no sound comes.

The moon has risen higher in the sky; its light
stripes the grey canvas of the set
with a grave motley. From these shades
a pageant of attendants form: tulle,
tutus, watery diamonds. The kings
dressed in old newspapers sit,
stony on a stone bench, monkey-masked.

*Poet:* 'What ho, a Watteau! Night
of masks and music, moony shine
replacing with oiled water (pitter pat)
the fairies' decandescence.'

The mothy figures start to fade.
The Princess is disclosed
as crumpled as a kleenex by the lake.

*Poet:* 'The hero has deserted her. The swans
mourn round her in a mob of lace, evaporate.
She droops; she fails. Will Tinker die
in all this vacant prettiness?
One sigh would resurrect the belle
with a small tinsel jingle!'

*Chico:* 'Come, come. I will refresh you.
What's the truth? Is Pierrot prince?
You, Pierrette, who only have
a thimble kiss,
will grow up to play mother to lost boys!'

*Poet:* 'But Wendy fades, Eurydice
who leads her hunters through the dark,
our evening star.'

49

The Captain rises, claps his hands.
Thin childish voices answer.

The little boys in their balloon
(a fire by night, a cloud by day)
sing their unworldly anthem.

False dawn, a clamour in the trees,
they draw the Princess after them.
They leave; she tags along.

Small water sounds. A Roland note (French horn).

*Poet:* 'That music is not mine
nor can I answer. Loneliness
overwhelms me like a thick disease.
I am untwinned, unwomaned, womanless.
And she was never part of me,
as fictive as a Leda's egg, as beautiful.

'I'm not at home in poetry.
The mockingbird
makes its loud noises in the leaves
(allusions, it's no plagiarist)
and treads its mate
and nests and rears its young – But I
am dumb, midnighted, and unpaged.'

He holds his hand out toward the dog
who comes to it, sniffs, ducks the pat,
and goes back to its post.

*III : i Anarchistic Naught Music*

The poet, dog, and stone kings stay.
The light recedes.
The plashing of the lake subsides.
The moon has drifted off,
leaving the sky less luminous.

Cymbals. A crash of metal. The Prince
in phosphorescent battle garb,
bright as a dragon, swaggers on.
Ignoring the Poet, he gives the kings
a courtier's bow (obsequious – and
arrogant).

*Prince:* 'All has been written as foretold.
        The teller's been paid half-wages. Yet
        Achilles' arrow's not yet spent
        and tortoise history creeps on.
        I must achieve my destiny!
                                I will accept
        all your conditions, Majesties: fish stories,
        maps, glossalia – the meaning matters little
        when it means
        me!' (The three kings bow, reseat themselves.)
                'When's the next swan?'

*Poet:* 'The vanity of any pure conception boggles thought.'

*Prince:* 'Do you deny the grandeur of my chords?
        I must embark! My music calls me forth!'

*Poet:* 'It does. The stage moves as you will,
        our middle world, this media.
        Obedient to your theatre, it may be launched.
        An ocean streams before you, world
        whose margin ever fades:
        to strive, to seek, to never find –

        'Write your white letter to the moon
        and wear it into battle! You'll survive.
        A cliché is unkillable!'

*Prince* (correcting): 'An archetype!' (Exits.)

## III : ii  Chicken Little's Hat Music

*Poet:* 'After him historians, bards, journalists,
you voters. He's your True North, fiction,
precedent! All your excitement's in his lies
which were, I think, at first my own.
I must disown him now he has
his other life.
Time will excuse, enoble him.

'I could write more, but all that's left is wars.
You love to read about them, so
I'll let you all imagine them.
You colourize the blacks and whites.
There may have been some greys,
or other colours. Blood. How should I know?
I hid.

'But now the election's made. The extra strings,
the second oboist, the harp,
all those excessive trumpets, have returned
for the finale. Now
the skying hero, heroine
have sung their final arias. Their crowns
mean dissolution. I outlive
my stories. In this place
I blow my whistle.
No one comes.

'I can't make up what isn't there. The sky
bears on its separating stream
the paper cutouts of the stars, pure heroines
and heroes, kings in putty, sheep,
lost children, birds, and governors
washing their hands.

'They sink into the scenery.
Nothing is left.
Like the last pig in the nursery rhyme,
I cry and cry.'

The three kings rise.

*Groucho:* 'Don't panic as life peters out.
    All history is juvenile, is storybooks.
    I set this into motion and let you,
    poor poet, prattle, but
    the sting's in the tail of the anecdote:
    the crocodile
    whose stomach clocks
    the one adventure: braving Dad
    (the ghostly Mr. Darling, one-in-three).

    'It's night. You can not read the dial:
    *Count, mortal, only the sunny hours!*'

The kings depart. From offstage, Chico's voice:

    'Unfeathered biped, emperor's robes
    are not as warm
    as swan wing, goose quill, chicken down.
    Make a warm nest.
    The winter howls around it.
    Nothing's safe.
    You could die here, a nothing, all alone
    strung out upon the stringing of your plot,
    but try your fairy whistle once again.
    You must believe.
    Believe!'

The curtain falls, the theatre grows dark,
the small, goat-footed collie takes the Book.

IV

## 'Come Up and Be Dead!'
– for Jenny Wren

'Come up and be dead!' the stars say, almost.
Lovely, profuse, anonymous.
So say the falls still falling as they leap,
and the grey-blue cliffs from which one bird,
a scuffed sea-eagle, looses and sets sail.

We need sometimes that lifting off,
as if we can not walk our course
unless some other carries us part way
at one with wing and current, wind and breath.

How could we have ever come down again?
The stairs hurt like a ladder's rung.
The roads foam with litter and snarling dogs.
Shadows livid with ruin glare
past us toward their mad purposes.

As if we swam, once, in an aether
nobler than this one; now,
crippled, we dance, in love
not with the star shine of the dead
but with the dogged faces of the street.
They draw us down.

## Everything's Just Fine

I have these great grotesque despairs
without a name to put to them.

They run around like dogs all tied
in one long leash about my knees
and trip me up, disgracefully, yapping
at anything. They do,
they do
yap

oh most fearfully.

I have no license for them. How
to buy the rightful owning
of an angst –

She was
a sort of friend
who stopped me in the mid-college hall and cried
'Pray tell me how is Desperate, Despair,
Grief, Fury, Envy, Hopelessness, and Pain?'

by what dog names
she called them.

What to say?
'Why everything is fine, fine, fine,'
I lied,
and ran away.

And yet their constant yelping keeps
someone awake.
Since they are yarded in my
self
I should, advisedly, shut up
all exits, all loud roaring paths
of sound, all close communicant
whine ways.

They bark. They bark.
The neighbours shun

my dogged daze.

## Music for a While

music can touch the gabby heart
as words can't do

a star
which has no music can exhaust
our speech

heaven casts its fiery spears in vain –
the children of the earth like corn
flourish in golden brevities

and something like a phoebe's note,
harsher, perhaps, in the August heat,
repeats, repeats

the woods are stuffed

the gods, for whom Bach, Handel, are but gnats
and spill their music like the foam
of some spent robin on the dusk –
the gods
may not exist

if music lapse, eternity grow bored?
'a cry in the streets' –

we must invent

a small bird calls in the great dark
say 'darkness is
God's listening'

say so

## Just Like That

It's not the wishing fails,
but breath

inhales –

and all things clatter by.

The clouds
collapse

on a poor chicken's head,
the acorn
of the universe

that was,
and is no longer.
Love

passes in an instant
like the snow

drops on green grass.

Amo, amas,

amavit –

Just like that.

## Triptych/Tock

i    *Emblem*

> The carts askew in the parking lot,
> > a lonely moon,
> > the Foodmaster store's
> > > > still open,
> > > its glass walls
> > lined with parcels and posters
> > and paper flowers.

> Under the token street lamp
> > a grey car
> sits, in its salt and sanded hide
> > an emblem of dailiness reserved
> > > for this dull twilight,
> > > > this sweatered moon,
> > > > > > > this
> > > tired
> > > > poet's mind.

ii    *Henny Penny*

No Heroine speaks for The Age or writes
the life and growth of The Poet's Mind.
Caucus: crows drowning the lesser birds,
    eggs riddled in nests.

> Where is the Female
> > Voice
> > > and must
> there be but One?
> Across the stages of the skies I see the gods
> > attended by handmaidens and handgods.

Outside, the trees
shake in a sexy manner their gold pods.
In the deep woods the fox recurs,
a narrative
preceding words.
Back home
the rooster writes his epic verse
to what he knows.

The hen
is never sure enough.
Even the worm at her springy feet
is something less uncertain, yet
the story will devour them both.
Slung over its back
all poultry is identical.
And worms.                    And verse.


iii   *Revision*

The beam that long held up the weight
of beds, books, bricks, and chimney piece,
all that swept clean, wrapped up, wheel-barrowed off,
is struck now with lightheadedness.
The cage
which kept a bird from harm, has been undone,
and like a bell without a tongue
frames emptiness.

Or you are like a boat drawn up on soil,
your planks struck through,
with nowhere left to go. The nails
that held you in your character

now fidget, rust; they would be gone
    like that freed bird, so newly wild,
    or those loud children, disembarked.

            You are not what you were.
            But redefine
        your strength, your open gentleness.
            Your structure now be narrative,
            a going forth!

## Bog Song

The quick bog stretches the universe,
fleshens the soul.
Bog song: daemons of fingernail,
marsh couplings, backs and elbows, nodes
that butt the heart along the shore
to creak like surf,

that out of the mud re-richened with the slough
of funeral extravagance,
the green brine clammy with new deaths,
boils the old cauldron,

the turtle shell
that floats upon the grainy mere
of animal, and bears
the angel, nude idea, self,
the integral bog rainbow –

That this flood,
this grapple grasp,
be covenant,
be even love!

## Ugetsu

'The fairies have no insides.'
But you don't
know that.

The town stinks of the war.
Death buzzes green as horseflies on her veil.

She might be the white pampas grass
by the silk lake,
or poetry;
she might be greed.

Her father's voice is sonorous
at that symbolic wedding art
constructs with life.
But crabs

ate him in some sea-battle long ago.
His ship was like a lanterned skull.
It vanished, cinder, in his wake.

Life writes a book against her, who
will weep, will wither,
will be grass
when life has burned her houses down.

In the real village of real wars
your murdered wife can not make love.
She sighs,
'I am your better half'

    to you, dead to all worlds,
sleep-numbed.

## 'Woman with Child'
– a Japanese print

He's a good little boy and will carry
the fan and the lamp of fireflies. She
has all the cumbrous layers of her dress
to tote ox-fashion: grey silk stuffed
with batting, red slip, folded blues
that drag upon the humid grass.
She holds her dress with two hands.
*See,* she says to the little boy
who sways his lights before him, makes
his tiny weathers flicker.
The flies will soon grow tired.
So will he. She'll have to carry him back home.
*See,* she is saying to him now. *See.*

## From the Wings

Tonight, that rose-pink scudding sky
whose navy clouds rush past the moon
    (exaggerated theatre whose one round eye
    stares blankly as a button) is
an overture
to some profounder opera than my own.

It reminds me that I am not here,
midcentre in your interests.
Out front an epic happens, not on me
    in my meek overcoat and boots,
    receiving what the weather brings,
    in this case, snow.

## About the Size of It

This man runs into the forest
breaking its red-tipped branches, flails
among the ice-encrusted leaves,
is,
he says,
the poet of himself.

He sees himself, his vividness
of shoulder, his strong arms,
as one with what he fractures. He
contains, he says,
what he has run inside.
Says 'Woods.'

Better he should go mousely; creep
flat as a dry leaf; write
on snow calligraphy
of his own diary doings; claim

only a single errand run;
report: one nut.

## Postcard from Yellowstone

This is the Muttering Mountain
coming alive in a hundred cracks
like Peer Gynt's palace, underworld
erupting into overworld –

There's a tiny shrine, a wood bridge,
a mud parking lot.
A rattler basks at the far end.
We were here.
X.

It doesn't show
those sapphire gentians or the crisp
denoting-bison-footprints where the crust
drooled into boiling liquid and gave way.

You have to be careful.
                    Love,

                 M

# Too Close for Comfort to the Text

O: sex? U: open. I: the finger without weight
(we all have ten).
X: fingers (hope? hypocrisy? a lie?).
T: levels out. o: dots the eye.
M: mouth that does not say.
E: teeth – a comb perhaps.
     (I do like Y: the U's closed tail,
     hanging in cuneiform debris
     like Alice's mouse's history.)
D: dubious (or not) – the tale has not
(O knot!) (not E) – A holds it, basic frame,
a starting point, you will need two
and one board in between (I comatose).
     (You can not build on S, C, Z –
     they wriggle out among your toes.)

Out of these inky sparrow tracks
make colour, motion, time
manoeuvering in its boughs small rain,
the evening drawing in, dull aches
of duller weather, lonesomeness,
a shutter banging in the wind, and memory,
in its hawsers, tugging free . . .

## 'Woman with Green Umbrella' by Van Gogh

The wind is horrid,
the moon is horrid,
the orange sky turns round and round,
and the trees are twisted tight as springs
and end in needle poodle knots
like threatening mops.

She holds
her green umbrella tight. They might
snatch it from her with their wild
thin fingers. Those stiff trees
might snap, go off in puffs of pain,
electric ecstasies as brief
as a quelled breath.

The orange sky spins.
She holds her green umbrella close.
It will not help.

# O

What was that? It came out of the sky
like a fried egg onto the green
grass, like an astral eye,
a yellow yolk eye pippin,
like a pie, or pi,
that round Greek thing.

The roundhead witness of daybreak,
gold aureoled sunflower, turns
her gape head in an O of awe.
Is this the thought
that holds her stamens to the dawn,
her pistils shot?

The daisy in the sky, round,
passionately dumb,
that crackles like the butter in a pan,
spitfire, has creased the glacier dawn.
She blacks its eye by closing hers.

Go, lovely weed.
Among the drying grasses fade
a century to the second, flare
a knot among the grasses. In this eye
was all that could exist, was all
continued to exist, was
alpha and omega, solitude.

Become the clenched bright yellow fist,
tomorrow's downhead baby. Blow
the parachutes of nothing to the air.
They land upon a thousand fields
in parodies of heaven. They dig in.
They will endure, fair thoughts
in a round maid's lap. Gold eyes.

# Katy's Cove

The whiteness of the stones
through which the water,
variously brown, green, and lilac,
like a fish insinuates its mindless ways,
effects the stoic brilliance of
a temple bleached by centuries.

It might have been the Aegean if
it weren't so cold.

The tourists shuffle from their bus
as gaudy as geraniums
toward the blue, chalky, canteen door,
and then out toward the white spit where
the stodgy lighthouse seems to knead
the water with its sphinx's paws.

It can, some days, be dangerous.
The sea can rise and slap you down
to be shoved up in a week or so
fringed like a hank of seaweed.

There's a white church built like an icehouse
whose sharp tip
seems like it might blare warnings.
And working dories, shuddering in their berths.

What is it like to be living here,
inside a snapshot, picturesque,
ignoring the tourists like the dull,
half-mirroring reflections on
a tank's glass wall
nudged by uninterested fish?
To be still here when the tourists go?

Among the massive boulder fields
the red haws of the beach rose glow.
People have always lived hereabouts.
It's been, always, cold.

## There Are Real Ants in the Metro

There are real ants in the metro.
I have sat all day
watching the tired feet go by
under the bank's glass forest
where tame trees shiver in tin can breeze,
always the same shiver, always the same breeze.

A ventral blast spouts from the metro's mouth.
On each ridge of the moving stair
rides a single ant. The concourse stinks
of candy, shoes. A soul drifts by
in a paper sheaf, green paper with a stapled top.

On the fourteenth floor,
drenched in livid lounge perfume,
a rigid light bulb dusts the hall.
The long shaft bellows: a trapped wind.

The workmen, seen from here as ants:
blond pigtailed, black t-shirted, jeans,
are not, mere ants, essential things.
They crawl out from their shaft at mezzanine.

Go down. The eye gets smaller.
Heaps, hills, vast caverns, anti-hills,
stone gardens, plastic rubble –
worm holes of the polis – the next train
carries an ant on its forehead
like a beam.

**Consider Briefly**


Consider this
          thing –

precise

as a milk tooth –
as the dab of 'blood'
on the bleeding tooth sea snail or on
the lip of the cat-faced orchid.

Consider, too,
the rasping tongue
of the voracious mollusc, or
the child's tongue, cherishing the gap,
or the cat's tongue,
or the nip
that severed the freckled petal.

Now
          it's time to put the cat out,
child to bed,
the sea shell back in the treasure box.

Time out's
          out.

## Seven Classical Chinese Pictures

I  Two birds look with suspicion at poetry.
Red leaves!

II  Grass, yes, and moon shapes.
A great many names over this poem.

III  A fine drawn word exorcises.

IV  Drawing a hundred times,
what is the shape of a willow?

V  Maple-leaved horses high striding –
orange-red, colour of dreams.

VI  I'm not high enough up. Mist
there. Two men.
Ox on the path.
Higher. No ox.
Higher.

VII  All my pots in a row.
You say they're persimmons?
No matter.

M. Travis Lane and her husband, Lauriat, came to Fredericton in 1960, shortly after the birth of their first child, Hannah. After the birth of their second child, named for his father, and the completion of Travis's doctorate from Cornell, the Lanes became Canadian citizens. Professor Lauriat Lane has recently retired from the Department of English at the University of New Brunswick, but Travis remains an Honorary Research Associate with the department. Travis's interests include Commonwealth literature and contemporary poetry in general, but her special interest is Canadian poetry, and she writes reviews regularly, many of which have appeared in *The Fiddlehead*.

The poetry of M. Travis Lane first appeared in *Five Poets* (Cornell, 1960). Since then she has brought out *An Inch or So of Garden, Poems 1968-1972, Homecomings, Divinations and Shorter Poems* (Pat Lowther Prize, 1980), *Walking Under the Nebulae, Reckonings*, and *Solid Things*. A ninth book, *Temporary Shelter*, appeared from Goose Lane Editions in 1993.